RUBES®
by Leigh Rubin

A Perigee Book

Perigee Books
are published by
The Putnam Publishing Group
200 Madison Avenue
New York, NY 10016

Library of Congress Cataloging-in-Publication Data

Rubin, Leigh.
  Rubes.

  1. American wit and humor, Pictorial.   I. Title.
NC1429.R775   1988   741.5'973   88-17851
ISBN 0-399-51488-0

Printed in the United States of America
1   2   3   4   5   6   7   8   9   10

For my wife Teresa and my son Jeremy

Other books by Leigh Rubin

Notable Quotes
Encore!
Amusing Arrangements
Sharks!...Are People Too!

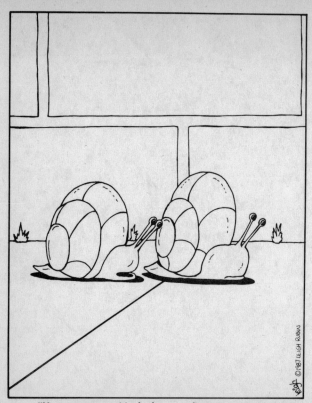

"Here we are, positively the most disgusting, repulsive, nauseating, slimy creatures ever to crawl on the face of the earth, yet people still consider us a delicacy. Where did we go wrong?"

SPEED ENFORCED BY AIRCRAFT

Morton's fear of the dentist was not completely
without justification.

"Remember, son, good things come to those who wait."

3

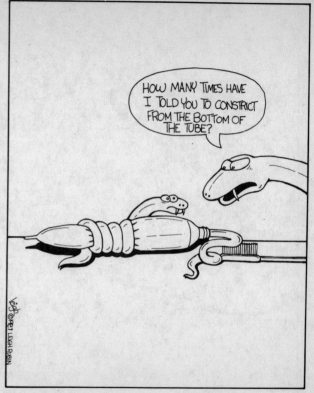

4

"Don't you ever wonder if there's
more to life than chasing the buck?"

"I'd like to call the House Committee on Ethics
to order, but apparently someone has stolen the gavel."

"Well, I see you're wasting another night
vegetating in front of the television!"

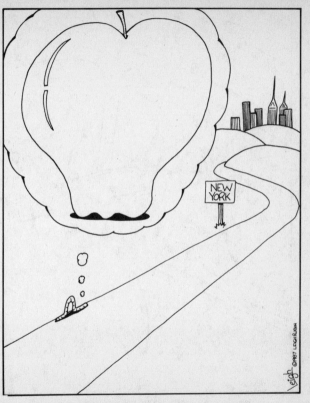

"My license, officer? Uh, Ha! Ha! I must have left it on my other collar!"

A day in Davy's life.

Dangerous parasites.

"...And this one is for having the most medals."

Unnatural history.

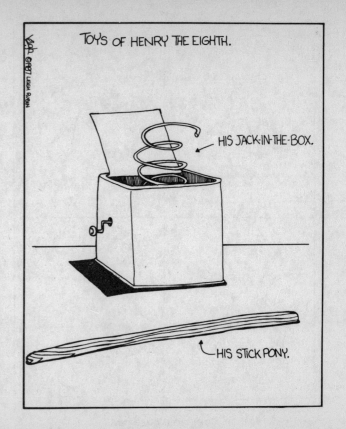

Methuselah, the smart shopper.

14

Foolish pride.

"My goodness, Frank, I wish you'd stop
constantly changing your mind!"

The detectives returned to question Tom Tom, the Piper's son. It seemed that certain inconsistencies in his original statement did not appear kosher.

Snail Scouts.

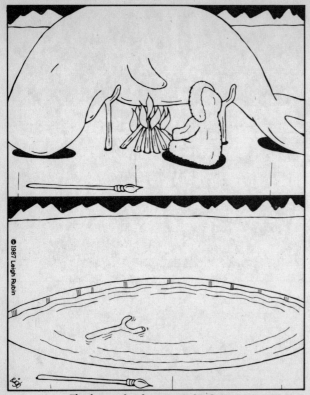

The hazards of an arctic barbecue.

"Listen, pal. Can't we act domesticated about this?"

19

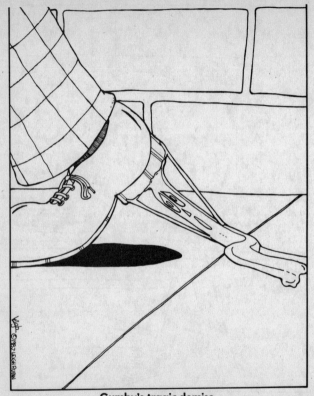

Gumby's tragic demise.

21

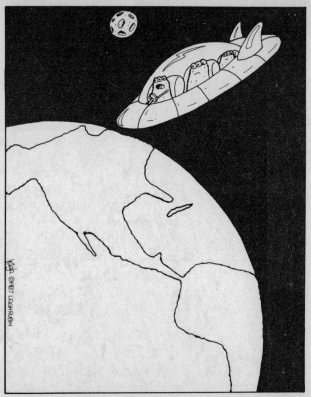

"Better lock the doors. This is a lousy neighborhood!"

22

Herbert waits in great anticipation for the denture fairy.

WHY THEIR HATS NEVER BLOW OFF.

Facts you need to know.

"Thank goodness...shade at last!"

"Five o'clock....Time to wrap it up."

"You heard me right, I said this cartoon ain't big enough
for the both of us."

25

"Now, observe carefully as I demonstrate the
'two birds, one stone' theory."

26

27

Naturally there was disappointment when the photos came back from the giraffe family reunion.

28

31

"Oh great! Your mother is coming over
and this place is an absolute sty!"

Calves can be so cruel.

Primitive, yet effective, giraffe catching techniques.

"Be a good little lamb and eat all of your grass
so you'll grow up big and strong and become a
seat cover like your father."

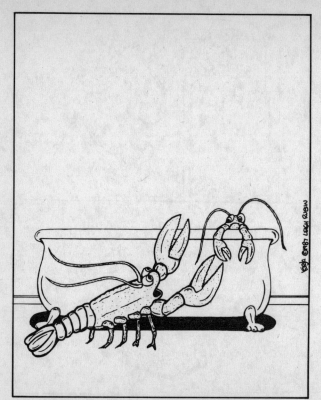

"Now remember, turn on the cold water first.
You know what happened to your father!"

"For crying out loud, would you get in here and cover up
these darn things so I can concentrate?"

36

"I'm tired of the singles scene...
men leering at me as if I was a piece of meat."

"I'm afraid a bulletproof vest is completely out of the question, old boy. Any other last requests?"

THE ABDOMINAL SNOWMAN

"Can't you wait to leak until we get to the next gas station?"

Shootout at the library.

**"Well, this is just great! The Gazelles cancelled dinner.
Now what are we going to eat?"**

"You never take me anywhere."

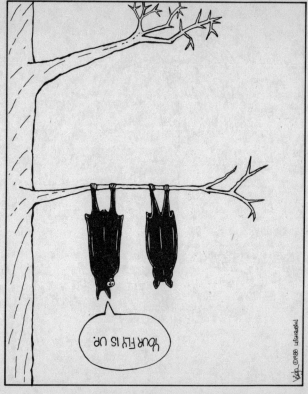

"Come wash up, dear...dinner is crossing the road."

"Momma! Momma!"

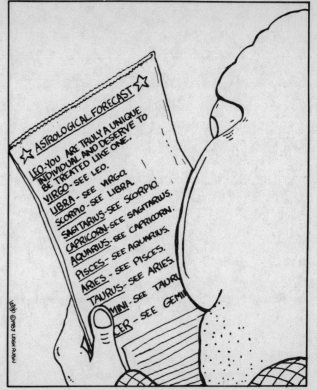

The original Teddy, bare.

"It's the police...your son King is in trouble again."

"Two cavities! That's it...no more peanut brittle!"

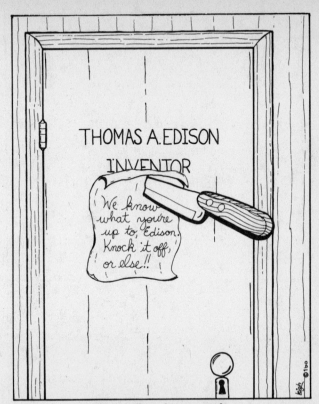

The candlemakers get ugly.

"Say, old boy... you in the mood to try something gnu?"

The Disney Channel.

"I know it's none of my business, señor,
but each cigarette is like another nail in your coffin."

"It was a stupid idea, Harry.
You just had to charge in and buy a convertible."

"Don't give me that 'I was out meditating with the boys' business. I know darn well you were down at the bar reaching higher states of unconsciousness with some cheap little devotee!"

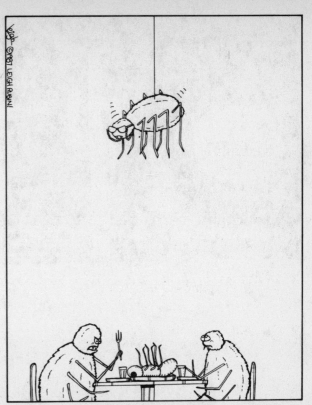

"Tell me, why is it that every time we sit down for dinner your mother drops in?"

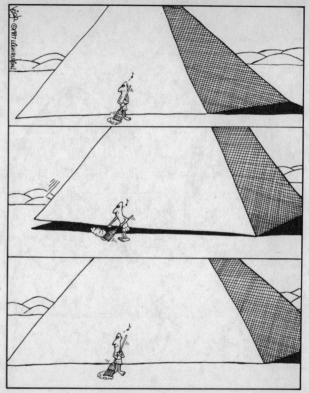

"Another sleepless night...maybe if I go terrorize some campers I'll get lucky and someone will shoot me with a tranquilizer."

The world's longest chess match between Vladimir Lipovitch and Ivan Zundorfski was disqualified from *The Guinness Book of World Records* when both players were discovered to be deceased.

"Remember this? Boy, that was some Thanksgiving!"

"What?! Are you kids crazy?! Don't you know it's dangerous to play in there?"

"It's my wife... She's been hibernating... with another bear."

"It's cool, guys, the cat's away."

On the lean beef ranch.

58

Early American indigestion.

"No, you may not wear lipstick! Number one, you're not old enough and number two, you don't have lips!"

Where non-fat milk comes from.

Al forgot to use his sunscreen.

The Pillsbury Doughboy meets his maker.

AND IF WE CAN'T LAUGH AT OURSELVES, WHO CAN WE LAUGH AT?

The Clown Philosopher.

"You, young man, are old enough to know better than to play with your food!"

Who does the baby resemble?

"Whew! You stink more than usual!
What did you have for lunch?"

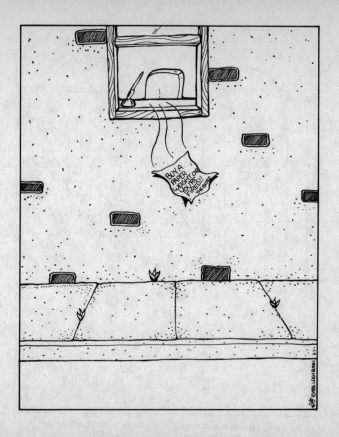

"This just in...ferocious escaped lion devours anchorman...details at 11:00."

Old MacDonald *had* a farm.

65

"Hello, Acme Pest Control? Come over right away...there's a large slug on my couch!"

Vanishing species.

"I was orphaned as a cub and never learned to hunt."

"Remember, amigo, aim for his body, the cape is just a diversion."

71

When mummies skinny-dip.

72

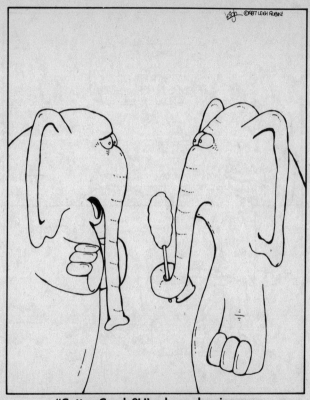

"Cotton Candy?! I've been cleaning my
ears with that stuff for years!"

No matter how hard he tried, he couldn't shake the feeling that his wife had been unfaithful.

"Now *those* are humps!"

Fresh fish.

Tanning hides.

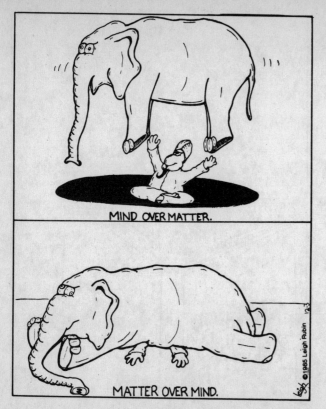

MIND OVER MATTER.

MATTER OVER MIND.

MOOD SWINGS

BE SAFETY CONSCIOUS

© 1987 Leigh Rubin

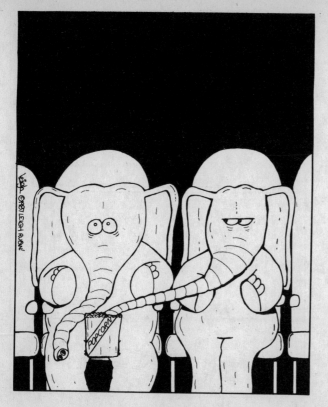

It was stripes as usual at the zebra fashion show.

"That does it, Leroy. Next time he don't get no last meal."

83

84

"That's him, officer, he's the one who killed my garden...I'll never forget those beady little eyes!"

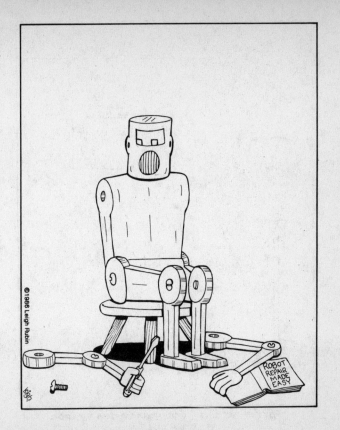

"For the last time...if you want a new fur coat, grow one!"

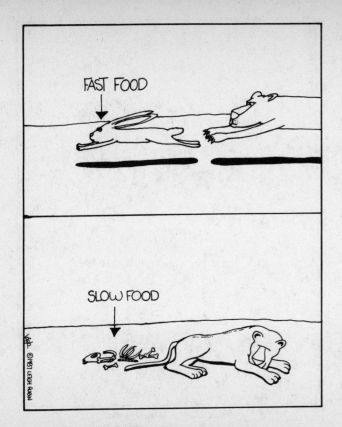

FAST FOOD

SLOW FOOD

EATH ROW

Fate prevented Norman Smith from completing the
last chapter of "How to Get Away with Murder."

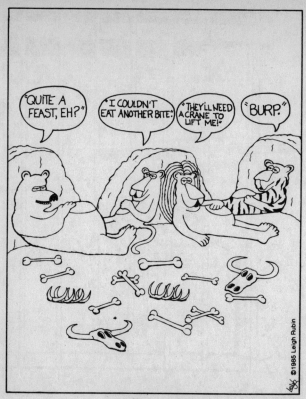

Stuffed animals.

**After Marcie leapt, Herb
realized it was just infatuation.**

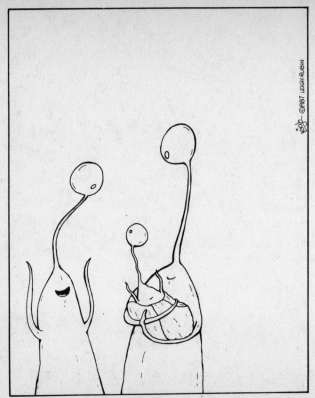

"Oh Martha, he's just precious!...and he has your eye!"

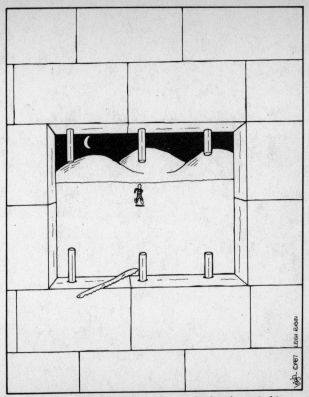

Milt would not be able to attend the luncheon in his honor, naming him "Model Prisoner of the Year."

91